Southern Poets

Edited by Aimée Vanstone

poetrynow

First published in Great Britain in 2007 by:
Poetry Now
Remus House
Coltsfoot Drive
Peterborough
PE2 9JX
Telephone: 01733 898101
Website: www.forwardpress.co.uk

SB ISBN 978-1 84602 065 0

Foreword

Although we are a nation of poets we are accused of not reading poetry, or buying poetry books. After many years of listening to the incessant gripes of poetry publishers, I can only assume that the books they publish, in general, are books that most people do not want to read.

Poetry should not be obscure, introverted, and as cryptic as a crossword puzzle: it is the poet's duty to reach out and embrace the world.

The world owes the poet nothing and we should not be expected to dig and delve into a rambling discourse searching for some inner meaning.

The reason we write poetry (and almost all of us do) is because we want to communicate: an ideal; an idea; or a specific feeling. Poetry is as essential in communication, as a letter; a radio; a telephone, and the main criterion for selecting the poems in this anthology is very simple: they communicate.

Contents

The Poems

Jersey Legend

Wave counterparts flash and burst
Just there, Grosnez Point, just west
Night shadows, a name from history unrehearsed
Have seen Celeste
Half heard, cloak by cloak
Dowse of daisies heads along L'etacq Point
Lost golf balls in Gorselane's yellow yolk
Atlantic's dark eye threshes St Ouen's break point
Redcoat's brother lost an eye
Higheavern, down gully, northern strip
We're still alive
May 1945
Two for the striped deckchairs
Summer's night auras, ripples of other flowers
Drizzle - dropped clouds, silver wind fanfare
It's Saturday again, shower
By the roots, roots, leaves, flat grass
Brightness to brightness
Gorse fire, aquamarine, stirs angels' eyes, stain-glassed
A golden evening, inherited mellowness.

Edward Tanguy (Jersey)

Second Post

He watches her carefully
His eyes handle her with care
With caring
He unwraps this precious moment

Layers of conversation
Like tissue paper
Are shrouding this breakable heart

They are carefully removed
Displaced
To reveal a thing of beauty

He reveals his heart

Her heart is already parcelled
In reams of brown paper and string
First Class delivery
To rough hands and tearing

But still

He watches her carefully
His eyes handle her with care
With caring
He unwraps this precious moment

Emma Ayling (Jersey)

The Cricket Pavilion

I remember the green grass, glistening in the morning dew light,
No longer in white, within in our view;
Yes I remember, because of that sunny afternoon,
That resounded leather on willow, on that hot summer day;
in late June.

I walked wet turf, my track reflected in that morning dew,
The green, glistening dew, compressed the depressed morning dew;
Meadowsweet, the green, fresh cut grass, is what I saw.
To be no more the community depleted.

Yes I remember, the reflection of that June afternoon,
Cucumber sandwiches; tea came so soon.
The shrill sound sonnet; the mistlethrush thrilled the air.
Whit was past; the day welcomed a lady fair.

The green grass glistens' no longer glorifying the morning dew,
The glow reflects on the memory of the glistening, green grass
with morning dew.
Glorifying the memory, mystifying the wet willow, that summer day.

Ann Hubbard (St Leonards-on-Sea)

Human Cocoons

Early hours in a London high street,
Before shops open their doors,
One never fails to see a few human cocoons.

A bulky blanket, a person in it,
Neatly in line with the doorway.
Cocoons hatch every day,
As shopkeepers reach the doors.

A person appears, un-metamorphosed,
Just as the night before,
Day after day.

Turning into a cocoon at night,
And hatching in the morning,
Unchanged.
What a destiny for the human-cocoons.

Yoko Hand (London)

Ashes

Dust to dust leaves a softer and kinder
Image than dull, lifeless, clinkery ashes,
Residue from once warm, glowing cinders,
Where too soon a flickering ember passes.
Life's frailty no more, now a free soul
Who needs to be with us in our sorrow.
His like can never more become a whole,
But his nearness felt in each tomorrow.
Now silvery dust settled near daffodils
In his garden, loved, tended for so long,
On him the sun will shine, the rain will fill
Silver runnels, birds serenade their song.
We'll remember him in each morning dew
And in the evening when the breeze nips through!

Pat Heppel (Plymouth)

Poetry

Thoughts tumble in my mind
do not lie fallow
dropped like young seedlings
into fertile soil,
received, rise up, are seldom dormant,
they are my dreams.
Some stay inside
forever cosseted,
wrapped in cocoon like secrecy
for they are too delicate
to venture onto paper
or to be read aloud.

Others are scattered
on bits of paper flying in the wind,
someone may pick them up,
make sense of senselessness,
take comfort from the knowledge
that somewhere else there is
someone seeking the same truths,
making the same mistakes,
as restless as the sea, the wind, as people.
The essence in the seed is poetry.
As our thoughts tumble into mind,
it cannot be by accident.
Will you not share your *passions* and ideas,
For poetry abounds in all of us.

Isabel Cortan (Bristol)

Village Cricket

In reminiscent haze he remembers the days
When, in his prime he batted; now, Panama-hatted,
He recalls that urge, the adrenaline surge,
When he faced the ball, answered the call
With ease and pleasure.

He's still quite fit - perhaps bent a bit,
Then, with a straighter back and bat - a different hat.
In flash-backs, he re-lives the attacks.
Past and present meet, the circle is complete,
He is still in the game.

And what of others? Wives and mothers?
Roped in to bake, make tea or cake?
They are watchers too.
Hoping the day is fine, that their lad will shine.
Sponging sprains, soaking stains -
The laundry-maid crew!

Needle venues, teams in the news,
Local fixtures; classless mixtures,
Foul weather or fair,
Dependable, indispensable,
Wherever the game, always the same
Supporters are there.

The opener takes heed, wary of youthful speed,
Then a change of style with spinning guile,
Or a bad call.
The fielder ready, alert and steady,
Throws in for the kill with unerring skill -
The bails fall.

Rain stops play; tail-enders save the day,
A miraculous catch changes the match,
Or bowler takes all.
Umpires, spectators, batsmen, bowlers, fielders
United with one aim . . . to play the game . . .
They have answered the call.

Pamela Courtney (Chichester)

The Forest Plain

Like bleached bones, picked bare
by carrion
lies driftwood spread across the plain,
an ancient field of battle
dulled and blurred by wind and rain.

Stands of trees survive and speak
to those
who have the means to hear
the spirit voices whispering low,
finding an understanding ear.

Horses huddle nose to tail
and shelter
from both heat and cold,
their ancestors would thus have stood
clinging on with tenuous hold.

Purple heather lights the way
and softens
lines too harsh to bear,
there is no red of blood past spilled,
nothing to taint the fragrant air.

Angela R Davies (Basingstoke)

The Joy Of A Summer Garden

The roundabout beauty
of damask roses,
flowering, magical, close.
A splash of colours
of the fuschia's trail
showing red, white and a blue pale,
drooping their heads
in sets of tubular bells.

Dainty, fluorescent, michelmas
Daisies, happy sitting on the borders,
In a merry display of colours,
Lovely, blue, forget-me-nots
Spreading their blooms upright -
Always mange to please a lot!

The pink carnations bring a
sweet scented feeling of
esteem, of perfection, of
nature so brightly
and to be free to wander in the
sun of summer is pure magic,
and is for any flower lover.

Sammy Davis (Bournemouth)

Easy Come, Easy Go

Life is cheap here -
And body parts too;
I'll sell you my kidney
To help me be able to buy some food to eat!

Life is cheap here -
Abandoned boys
Labelled for life and tortured in cells
Behind closed doors
Or disposed of for a small price.

Life is cheap here -
Children kidnapped
To work in mines . . .

Can't anyone see
That something needs to change?
Or will all this just remain
And remain
Indefinitely
While NGO's and volunteers
Mop up the pieces
In seemingly microscopic refuges?

Easy come, easy go
I know the world is not perfect
But how can a country
Go on like this?

N Jagger (Godalming)

Eastbourne

Split open the pod of the town
the belly of the good life and
the underbelly of crime.
Stately and Godly matrons,
rotund councillors of the EBC.
Over 60's visitors arrive in coaches
for their winter spree.
Children piling into parent's cars
twice a day from school,
shopkeepers, hoteliers and road sweepers,
the Big Issue of homeless people
standing in doorways with rugs and dogs.
In the small hours, clubs close,
tempers flare, a look or a stare
may end in a fight.

Elizabeth T Jenks (Eastbourne)

Treasure In Abundance

Life can be hard with a pace so brisk
That care must be taken to avoid any risk.
With a concentration set on daily routine
One can lose sight of the wider scene.

Time should be taken to escape our self-inflicted bounds,
Just to observe the beauty of our surrounds.
Our England has been extolled in verse many times
And to miss its charms is an inexcusable crime.

You lift your eyes and without fail, you see trees
Of all varieties, colours and sizes, swaying in the breeze.
Different shades of green, foliage amass
Blending in with similar characteristics of grass.

In each season this background is illuminated
By the various floral displays freely concentrated;
A riot of colours with a verdant backdrop
Shifting shades and tones with each season's crop.

Seize your opportunities while you may,
Nature freely gives you this choice every day.
So don't waste this chance of pleasure -
Look up and count your treasure.

Allen Jessop (London)

Secrets

He moved on quiet feet through the woods
Listening to the whispers of the old gods
He nodded to the friendly trees
And filled his head with the brown scent
Of moist, dark mould that cushioned his feet
And then
He saw a rag of reddish-brown fur
Caught in the claws of reaching thorns
Thorns that had torn it from the coat
Of a night-creeping fox that had low whimpered its loss
What a prize it was for a man who collected such things
He released it
But carefully
From the gripping thorns
And placed it in the warm, safe dark of his pocket

The man bowed to all after that
And returned to his familiar room
He removed the fur that had softly moulded to his pocket
And took from a secret place
A carved wooden box
And there he placed the fur
Placed it with a curious bone
A feather
The tooth of a dog
A smooth black stone
And other magic things
All that
Because he walked out one autumn morning
One toadstool morning
With the leaves falling
And a mature sun softly shining.

John Jones (Chelmsford)

Woman 2 Woman

Woman, what is this business of being
fearfully and wonderfully made?
Is it more than beauty, more than race, education,
motherhood and softness?
What do you know of being made in the image of your Creator.
How often during your busy days
do you take time out to acknowledge this?
What images do you hold, is it one of being tired,
washed up, abused, unheard,
Or bright, carried on wings, blessed, joyful,
saved by grace, beautiful, listened to by God?
Surely you must know by now, every morning you wake up,
In all situations, under every possible circumstance,
that you are part of and can depend on God.
Why else would he make you in His image?
Morning by morning, new mercies you see,
because your Maker causes this to happen for you.
Just you, especially you, the beautiful you.

God, the good, powerful, wonderful essence of life is always within
you, always around you, holding and lifting you up.
The essence and energy of God is what you are.
You can always depend on the living God.
The very life of God within you.
God, your God is the spirit of life.
It is not what we live, it is what we are.
Therefore, there is nothing so wrong that it cannot be put right,
Nothing so heavy that it cannot be lifted.
Nothing so horrible, heavy, deep, bad,
that you cannot work it through.
Move around it, step over it.
Pray it through, pray it through, pray it through.
Believe that you have the life of God within you.
It makes all things possible.

Before you get to believing how wonderfully and fearfully
you are made, you may need a spiritual diet,
A tablespoon of forgiveness
A whole heap of surrender
Daily prayer (early morning)
A good dose of gratitude
A shower of faith
Several bites of the word, to learn, patience,
gentleness, service and love
Washed down with courage and confidence in your Maker.
You see, you may have been filled up with so much of the weight that
does so easily beset us, that you have not had time to shed them and
see the beautiful you.
Just remember that He as promised you in His word
that He will never leave you nor forsake you.
He has called you by name and you are His,
made in His image, wonderfully and fearfully.

Dalia Alexander (Thornton Heath)

Souvenirs

Just another piece of bric-a-brac
A dust collector they think to them selves
Another to add to the collection
Only this time it's coloured glass.

They are right
You are a dust collector
But I dust you lovingly.
To me you are beauty, elegance,
Sunlight and warmth, creation
Of the skilful craftsman.

Red glass swan
In your chiselled beak
I see the long-armed firing iron
In your vermilion body
I see the fired furnace
From which you sprang.

Venetian phoenix
In your glass, tufted crest
Slim curve of your graceful neck
I see the smiling gondolier
I hear the waters lapping.

Just another piece of bric-a brac
But I dust you lovingly
An oh, how I remember Venice
City of love, of wine and beauty.

Kathleen Allison (Northolt)

Scenic Miracles

The grey mantle of winter's icy blast,
Shrouds fields and woods with intimidation,
Howling, haunting winds that bite the land,
Ignite the senses and stimulate imagination.

Elongated, sombre nights of winter's hush,
Evoke yearnings for release and liberation,
Breathtaking beauty evident, and soon we'll see
Longer days and the glory of spring's intoxication.

Emotional effects of winter's gloom are profound,
Remoteness and rawness obscures gratification,
Treasures are diverse and abundant, look around,
Problems dwarfed by nature and her miraculous manifestations.

Icicles sparkle like diamond chandeliers,
Snowflakes softly shimmer in lace decoration,
Robust little robin fluffs up against the chill,
Sturdy, resurgent snowdrop pierces the soil in jubilation.

Moonlight's luminosity triumphs over dark nights,
Star-studded skies twinkle with magnetism,
Startling sunsets follow days of fiery dawns,
A captivating canvas of constant transitions.

Each moment we should enthusiastically embrace,
The splendour of nature's undeniable resilience,
Seasons alter but the unending passage of time
Continues to radiate blessings of prodigious brilliance.

Celia Auld (Ashington)

Africa At War; Flight From Danger

Straggling, dusty, tired, along the rutted road
Hundreds drag themselves with sightless courage
From nowhere to nothing, crops and homes destroyed.

The rain so long delayed begins to fall
In torrents, warm and cleansing, settling the dust,
Turning the dry, sun-baked and ruthless road
Into red and sticky, clinging, sinking mud.

The bedraggled, unkempt line of refugees
Drags onward to an unknown distant land;
Many dangle sodden bundles at their sides
Not bearing them with jaunty pride upon their heads.

Dark night approaches and the sorry throng
Collapses on the bullet-spattered road;
No crumb to ease their gnawing hunger pains
And the rain holds out a mocking remedy for thirst
To people with no strength to offer up their tins.

The chilling torrent beats with cruel force
Upon the jaded and emaciated crowd;
They close their eyes but they can only sleep
In restless, nightmare snatches.
Mothers try to feed and warm their keening babes
Clutched against their frozen, empty breasts
As the infants' pleading slowly dies away.

At dawn's first touch of light some rise to meet
Another hostile day, trailing, unrested to erase
A paltry measure in the transient, early cool;
Others lie inert in blissful peace,
Women cradling silent children in their scraggy arms
And men released from worry for their starving kin.

As the rising sun points up the diminished line
A young one falters; takes her mother's hand;
As a burst of coughing gunfire drowns her whispered words
Her frenzied mother throws her to the ground.
The little girl, confused and terrified,
Hides her trembling body in a threadbare cloth;
Her mother drops beside her and the child
Huddles closer, seeking comfort from the noise
But her mother is no longer there; her life has flowed
With the blood that bubbles from her punctured head
And the quivering child stares blankly at the empty dawn.

P Edwards (Bath)

Forever Scotland

'Twas many a long year my Bonny Lass that I kissed you by the burn,
that gentle, flowing time - so long ago.
The servant hills, with the company of sheep, and the wreath-headed mountains of mists and billowing skies.
The loch so fine, stretching like a long arm to the glen,
The ragged robin unfurling her tresses,
and the wild heather blowing to the *winds of time.*
The plaintive cry of the gulls on the moor,
Clad with stones of ages gone.
Where clans of men fought their battles proud,
and pipers played their lamented tunes.
We come again to this place, with our love of so long ago,
My Bonny Lass, so weary now,
To capture the ties that bind it,
will it be the same now as it was then?
My love will last as long as the heather grows,
and the mountains *peak* to the sky,
Times of old, as is now, is forever Scotland.

Olivia Hicks (Bath)

Romans

The Romans journeyed on the Fosseway
To places on the southern coast
Their route passes my dwelling
And I hear their heavy footfalls,
Their presence is compelling.
Some must have died en route
Their souls still remain here.
My flowers lower their heads
And birds sing hymns of loss
These Romans go on marching
Forever on the Fosse.

Joan R Gilmour (Bath)

A Special Boy (A Boy With Autism)

He hears my voice
but I speak too loud
I disturb his thoughts
with a tone and pitch
that crashes through his mind
a mind that silently cries out for quiet.

He needs order, he needs numbers
number order
he needs times, places
what will happen next, how long will it take
and when is it time to go home?

But he is smart
he thinks that because he is special
he does not have to do
what everyone else does
he thinks he can play
by his own rules.

So he will make loud noises
when he should be quiet
and lay on his back to sleep
when he should be sitting
he rushes out of the doorway
when he should be working.

I whisper so that my voice
does not crash into his mind
but I know that my voice is like a vice
restricting his freedom
to daydream, his freedom
to be in a world separate from me
and everything that hurts his senses.

Helen Thorn (Bath)

Inner Space

The sweeping sun shone
Over my face
Why do I feel
So out of place?
I long to hear
The morning bird song
In some tranquil
Inner space
Moving along
Out of this rat race.

Linda Jones (Bath)

Journey

Falling, tumbling, spiralling
from the dark sky,
you fall into my lap,
I begin to heal.

Gently, soothing, coaxing,
eyes darting, mind chaotic,
brooding black, burst of red.
Patiently I sit and wait.

Pacing, shouting, clenching,
sitting, closing, ebbing,
Questions, intentions.
Calmly I journey with you.

Drained, tired, resigned.
Eyes imploring.
Finally exhausted.
Rest, head in my lap.

Samantha Seward (Newbury)

Painted Eyes

The gnome in the rockery sits peaceful and pensive,
And sees through painted eyes plum trees,
Flowering, laden with fragile, lacy pink blossom.
And he's noting too a hundred brilliant bouquets of spring splendour.
Pale petalled primroses, pansies of soft, purple velvet,
Rising fragrance of blue hyacinths, 'neath the shadow of red tulips,
Swaying, shining, meditating ferns in shaded greenery,
The painted eyes twinkle merrily in the sparkle of golden sunbeams,
As the gnome in the rockery sits, peaceful and pensive.

Maureen Plenderleith (Bristol)

The Minnie Master-Singer

In 1984
Was it Orell by the score?
New adventurer of rhyme,
Was so little said before?
Oh so little done before,
Reason and the New York Times;
Equal shares , artistic wars;
Poet, prophet, dame or dime.

Love is somehow insincere, poorly lit,
The Bridge of Sighs a good example
Of a laughing-weeping fit.

And there's a little ditty they re singing in the city,
And it doesn't matter to me if you sing along,
And it won't really matter if you love me long,
By Welsh daughter
I would sit momentarily.
Botticelli would have made you
Want to sit
In black and white and be
The harlequin of Times obituary.
Down littered streets to Merton's saintly crew
Stands love-in season, undramatic, tall.
Briefly remembered piping among the dead;
Nothing need be said.
The human psyche is sorting out, overseas,
What our New Year's resolution will be.
As year to year the art of delicate friends,
Picking or arranging flowers nicely,
Destroys desperate souls,
Desires Earth, fire, water snow.
A sterner beauty that the great Tom Bell,
Is making bird-breaking April lift
A greater glory than original sin.

Whichever century whispers of immortality,
Times martyr'd memorial marks, Uncertain City,
Three fawke-like burning figures of fun,
mortality,
Has thought up many ways to puzzle progress;
And so it continues:
Virgils undergraduate, drawing home.
Asia Minors civilisation.
Elation, and recession, and fatigue,
Simultaneous passions mix eventually.
(One ashy line from
Queens collective show.
Nature owns an enviable night-gown).

I understand, breaking all the usual seals,
How Saxon abbeys dominate past memory,
How Magdalens supreme monastic air
Was breathed by Wolsey, Wilde,
how bill-addressed,
Without your map, no tour would be complete.
God bless young Waugh (wherever he may be).
And freshman wearing brogues and rough tweeds.
An excellent bow-side oar or opening batsman
And travelled distant readers of Chapmans Homer.

And I shall cast a backward look (each way).
Oh absent heart grow fonder weak days.

Because sky-lit, clipped Gothic, half-armoured,
God bless you most of all the Radcliffe camera.

Neil Gooding (Bristol)

A Few Lessons in 'Bristle' Speak

Living in Bristol it's a must you see
To learn the *bristle* speak.
Dialects are strange but key
And certainly unique.

The 'good idea' of the Bristle chap
Soon becomes 'good ideal'
But don't you worry and don't you flap
As soon it won't seem surreal.

'Ees as ard as nails ee is'
when he thinks he's tough,
while your girlfriend carries her 'ambag',
and the dentist looks at your 'tuff' in a huff.

Don't forget your food's 'gert lush'
But never become a 'gert swellead'
Always ask 'Muh for you breckfuss'
And then ask 'ow bist' once you've been fed.

'Shut them bleeden doors, I's shrammed in yer'
Is often heard the cry.
This soft, west country burr,
Is wonderful, you'll sigh.

'Watch ar Muh's best chinawl!'
Is easy to understand!
And pretty soon you'll be able to call
Your baby your 'babber' in Bristle land.

'Awlright me luvver, ain't seen you frages'
to greet a long lost friend.
And once you've reached this mighty stage
Your learning's almost at an end!

Pamela Sears (Bristol)

The Street Called Straight

In Bristol there a Straight Street,
Not very long, though may have been longer in the past;
Warehouses turned into department stores,
With a car park at the end.
Slightly off-centre, separated from the main shopping centre
By a dual carriageway; how many people even know it is there?
How many people, who do go that way,
Know what the street is called?
Having noted its significance
In the hustle-bustle of everyday life?
I don't know how old the street is,
But I do know it is not the oldest with that name.
That honour belongs to a street in Damascus,
The oldest inhabited city in the world.
At least two thousand years old,
Where a man called Judas lived, who
Received a certain visitor; not welcome,
As he was a notorious terrorist,
Noted for hounding Christians
And sending them to their deaths.
No, this visitor was not welcome,
But Judas had received instructions from Above
And had to obey, no matter what the consequences.
His guest arrived, blind, disorientated,
And certainly not the man Judas had heard about.
What had become of the arrogant, sanctimonious,
Super-choleric Pharisee from Jerusalem, whom everybody feared?
Something about a blinding light, questions about persecuting God?
Broken wasn't the word for it; humiliatod, perhaps?
Anyway, his sight had to be restored,
A new name given, a fresh start,
Instruction given in the new Faith, then
Paul was ready to step out into the world.
There is a street in Bristol called Straight,
Newer, probably shorter than the original;
Certainly not as famous; but then, it's not every day
A dramatic event like that happens, is it?

Kathy Rawstron (Bristol)

My Special Place

Cornwall
This land of granite cliffs, surrounded by the sea.
Where gulls and kittiwakes soar overhead
And fulmars swoop for fish in deep, blue seas,
Where golden sands stretch out for miles and miles
Or nestle between rocks in sandy coves,
And fishing boats tie up to harbour walls
For safety, when a winter storm blows up.
Where one day skies are blue and high and clear
And little waves lap softly on the sand,
The next, tumultuous seas come crashing on the shore,
And surfers bravely ride the white-topped waves.
This place where red valerian grows beside the road
And honeysuckle and wild rose festoon the hedge,
Offering sweet nectar to the butterflies and bees.
A landscape full of long-deserted
Engine houses, monuments to men -
Who lived and died mining the tin and copper ore,
That once made Cornwall such a rich and famous place.
This land of song and music, male voice choirs,
Brass bands and festivals, of saints and myths
And legends, and of smuggling and wrecks.
This little part of England, quite unique,
So different in its own particular way,
My special place, from where my forbears came.
My heart is here - Cornwall my home.

Ann Linney (Redruth)

Cornish Riviera Express

Leaving the noise of Paddington station
The train seems almost a tranquil resort.
Rattling through grey back to back of suburbia
Eager for space where sea meets the sky
Reaching the Tamar, a warm glow fills me,
As we clatter across Brunel's fine bridge -
Westward to Cornwall, the place I call home.
The train slows down, a more reverent pace.
Emerald hills roll into the distance,
Deep, wooded valleys wind down to the sea.
Buzzards float high above on the thermals,
Rabbits abound in the fields with the sheep.
Truro's three spires watch over the city,
Signal the journey is soon at an end.
On past the mine stacks, legacy of tin,
Lending distinction to Cornwall's skyline.
At last St Michael's Mount is in sight,
Rising majestic'ly over the bay,
Where glistening water reflects the sky
And the view goes on for ever . . .

Anne Lawry (Penzance)

Upon Westminster Bridge (204 Years Later)

I stood, where he once stood, upon the city bridge,
And London passed me by, beneath a snow-filled sky.
Yes, boats, towers, domes and theatres still stand as once before,
But now there are new sights . . .
Cars, red buses, black taxis, motorbikes and other noisy signs
of 21st Century life.
And people walk and talk, not only to each other
but with mobile phones clamped to their ears,
Or listening to their iPods, blocking out all other sounds.

And there, to the right of the bridge is a new tribute to this age,
They call it *the London Eye,*
And it turns slowly with all its engineering genius for man
to ride up high on,
Up there you can see this splendid city sprawling out before you.

And as I stand upon this bridge where he once stood,
I know that some things have changed
and that some things never change,
And as the Thames continues on its path upstream,
I know that is the way life will always be . . .
Some things are timeless.

Jane Wade (Penzance)

Desmond

never played football
on school playground tarmac
with the boys,

or ran races trying
to beat the sou'west wind
with his class mates,

he held court,
sat on the only dustbin
in the school yard
going on and on
about his bus conductor ambition.

Desmond knew every bus stop
on the three different routes
between Falmouth and Penzance,
he could quote, fares, timetables,
regulations, bus and route numbers.

After school Desmond changed
into a bus conductor's uniform
to punch his ticket collection.

At weekends he built buses
from Meccano sets with lights and bells
that worked and a mirror on the stairs
to check the upper deck.

School sports days
were different, teachers
made Desmond enter every race,
he ran like a *long dog*, winning easily.

Desmond could have beat
the sou'west wind, instead
when he left school he made the buses run to time.

(Long dog - Cornish dialect for greyhound)

Les Merton (Redruth)

The Skateboarder

He boards the bus - nonchalantly,
his beloved board clutched to his breast;
a lithesome young Adonis of teenage years.
Faded blue jeans, sag well below his crotch
and concertina down toward white trainers,
with laces trailing.
He does not hear; spurns the world about him,
his ears accommodating those tiny ear pieces
so beloved by his generation, connected as
they invariably are to a 'music' provider
and from which those close to him can only
discern a constant, rhythmic beat' that of
a cymbal or some other like-sounding electronic
device, music of the spheres mayhap?
Straight strands of flowing, blond hair partially
cover these ear pieces, descending toward the
nape of his neck; a natural blond or from a
cosmetic container? It's hard to tell.
The bus jolts - brakes suddenly, his board
slips from his grasp, clanks to the floor;
those passengers nearby look in his direction
as he retrieves his cherished friend and slips
it between his knees, held in a tight grip,
thus ensuring that another slip will not occur
again; that distraction of others but of which
he is totally oblivious.
A bell rings, a sign indicates 'bus stopping',
it was not the callow youth who had pressed
the button but some other, he does however rise
from his seat in an almost trance-like movement,
listening still to who knows what, as tightly once more he hugs his
board against his plain
nonedescript tee shirt - and alights.
Did Olympus or some other more earthly tarmacked
mound here in Cornwall beckon him; not so much to
ascend some summit - the home of gods, but rather
to descend on that wheeled device which is his
obvious god, his only true friend, his skateboard!

Peter Mahoney (Hayle)

Nothing Stays The Same

As a child I sang about April Showers
bringing forth May flowers and with a
soft, warm breeze,

Flaming June meant that summer was truly here,
but nothing stays the same, we have
bitter winds and chilling rain in the merry
month of May.

What a shame that nothing stays the same
now, we have global warming with daffodils
peeping from the ground in March and all
gone in April, that was once full of promise.

Just like me, for once I sprang into spring
and looked to the future full of hope.
Now I live in the world of today, in the
wintertime of my life, which has arrived to
keep me company in the merry month of
May and nothing will ever be the same again.

Julia L Holden (Braunton)

Centuries Have Unfolded

Live life in the present.
It's all you've got.
Treasure each moment.
Don't hold onto hopeful yesterdays
and futures you'll never have.
It's time to let them go.

A river could run through
the time spent wasted
mulling over past joys and losses.
They mean nothing now.
Only the present is true
and cannot lie to you.

Forgotten faces, leave forgotten.
Pack them away in your briefcase
and mark 'do not open'.
Discard the key to your safe deposit box.
Burn old love letters.
They're not worth the paper
they were written on.
They didn't mean those empty words
or else you'd still be with them.

Today is precious.
Tomorrow may never come.
If I die next week, next month, next year,
Today, I don't want to be glum.

Andy Botterill (Exeter)

For Suzi

The last flickering embers of your soul
Twinkled across that hall
From deep, fathomless depths
That drowned your sight.

A dreadful fear swamped your features,
I knew you were near the end
And we stretched forward hands of friendship
Hands drenching you
With hope and faith
Care and love.

Pulling you into our life raft,
Herding you safe within the fold -
Free and clear of the soul-freezing,
Esteemless, shark-infested oceans
Of a lifetime of ruptured emotions.

Ian Burnett (Winkleigh)

Harmony

A racialist situation
has occurred on the beach
because when the sun is shining
all the pebbles are bleached.

When the sky is overcast
and white horses force their way
all the pebbles are brown or black
and in that colour stay.

Pure white as the driven snow
a sight to behold.
A mineral conglomeration
with many a story to be told.

They are a secret army
that move in stormy seas.
They mix together peacefully
each other to please.

Perhaps a lesson from the beach
could be taught throughout.
As there are no fanatics
to cause an unwanted rout.

Whatever the weather
whether black, brown or white
they are an example of harmony.
Could we learn? We might.

D R Thomas (Ottery St Mary)

Poole Harbour

Massive, safe haven from the westerlies,
Bounded by the rolling cliff-top downland,
Dotted with five varied islands,
Each with their own individual offering.
One shelters the shy red squirrel,
Deer swim over to enjoy its grasslands,
Woods and cliffs saw the start of scouting.
Probing the secrets of the Earth,
Another yields the black treasure of oil.
Lagoons offer feeding and protection
For flocks of over-wintering avian visitors.
Stands of rushes line the river banks.
There families of swans, ducks and scuttling moorhen
Nest to safely rear their young.
Deep channels filter in the sea craft,
Tankers, freighters and the ferries
And fishing boats in successive generations -
With the sleek lines of the mighty powerboats
And their wind blown cousins of the sail.
Over all the movement
One senses the ghosts of history;
The gathering of invasion forces,
Sturdy cod ships from Newfoundland,
Roman galleys with their slave propulsion,
Settlements of the skin-clad men.
This is busy, functioning Poole Harbour
Where past and present mingle.

Di Bagshawe (Poole)

Purbeck Path

Somewhere among the lonely hills
I steal along a secret track
That strays deep-fringed with buttercups.
Their golden heads gleam in the grass
And stretch in shining, wind-swept swathes
Where, distant from the busy world,
They raise their petals to the sun,
And shimmer on the shoulders of the hills.

Somewhere in lazy twists and turns
The path dips down to meadow lands
Where milkmaids and lush grasses grow.
High overhead the skylarks sing
Their litanies in sunlit skies.
Chords of loneliness and love
Stir the heart with sudden pain
Which softens gently in a mist of tears.

K Merle Chacksfield (Swanage)

Water Bottles

Best thing in the universe
Water that cleanses the body
Gives your taste buds a freshener
Hydrates you instead of dehydrate
If you run out
Pop into a shop
Buy another - never need be without water
Tap water is good
Have a water bottle at the ready
Tastes good when left in the fridge
Overnight
This is an innovation intention
Keep the water flowing
The earth solution to health and fitness
Water in the past was drunk - *tap water*
A water fountain in school
But wow! did we adults as kids miss out
Wouldn't do without a water bottle
At the ready now
Still water is the best
And the healthiest -
Let's hope there's no drought.
The Earth's solution to health and fitness
Water in the past was drunk - tap water
A water fountain in school
But wow! did we adults as kids miss out
Wouldn't do without a water bottle at the ready now
Still water is the best
And the healthiest -
Let's hope there's no drought.

Josie Lawson (St Leonards-on-Sea)

Room

Row of stark
Iron bar cages
At the end
The room where
Crucifixion like
People are killed.
Lethal violator
Veins the trembling
Form, gasps, pain in
Full view of others.
State sanctioned murder
The architect of this holocaust
Is ignorance, eyes
Not wanting to see
Ears not wanting to hear.
Screams from desperate ones
Who for many years have
Seen the slow inner death.
Only a raging anti-Christ
Would
Call his killing lust justice
No, this is not the way -
If hard questions are never asked
Answers will never be heard.

George Coombs (Hove)

Untitled

I have no room
for me
in myself
so I'm staying
with someone else
to find my place
on the little piece
of space
belonging
not to me.

Piotr Gabryelski (Cheltenham)

London Underground

Slogging down the murky past
Elephant and Castle at last
Digging deep into the earth
Ground zero maybe tomorrow
Sheltered from the weather
Hey Joe! This is forever
Hammersmith and City Line
Across to Covent Garden
Night attire sweet and sharp
Made your mark
Caught the tube at 6 am
Up early with the lark
Stand and deliver
Meet you in St James' tube station
Wearing a silk, blue scarf
Hat of finest cloth
Suited well for celebrative occasions
Marks the turning point in life
Caught the London Underground
To Knightsbridge, praise be!

S M Thompson (Southampton)

Untitled

There was a chink in the curtain.
A grey, misty dawn was breaking
But it was still dark.
The light was shining steadily on the chapel wall
Encouraging early prayer.
I crept across the room and peeped out.
A sister was approaching, scurrying across the garden,
Clutching something
On her way to join the others.
Just enough time to shower and belong.
The five minute bell rang.
I rushed across the garden
But they were singing
And I dared not interrupt
So I stood with my back against the wall.
And listened.

Annie M Rawsthorne (Aldershot)

Boxing Day 1975

You were slashed from my bloated carcass
soon after your clamour of distress
aborted your father's poetry reading
your entrance unseen. Pneumonia

has barred me for three whole days.
Why so difficult to breed a girl?
Wheeled in, still hamster-cheeked,
I crumbled beneath your soothsayer's stare.

When I leave you to sheathe your scrawny limbs,
and we creep back in the middle of the night,
terrified that you are not going to make it,
we find you leading

a post-puerperal choir, upstaging
Fifty Ways to Leave Your Lover.
The scar oozes for months, refusing to heal;
your flint pulverises my sandstone.

Carole Alexander (New Milton)

Broken Beauty

That day, that journey -

Everything we did, each one of those
Tiny decisions - everything following
From everything else -

Everything we did took us to the time
We were driving back, he and I
From a shopping trip.

Parallel lives . . .
We were driving back home.
Having braved the storm, the wind -

One could hardly walk outside
Without fighting it.
Chaotic and dangerous day.

Everything we did -

We hesitated at the last traffic lights.
Slowed down unnecessarily.
Everything we did after greeting the dawn

Took us to a single moment . . . in time
When the wind coldly mutilated
A tall tree growing by the roadside.

I saw the huge branch fall.
Broken beauty, it happened so fast -
Frighteningly quickly.

The branch fell in front of our car -
So close.
Everything we did

Took us to that single moment . . . in time.

Claire-Lyse Sylvester (Fleet)

Exile

Everything much smaller this April
Daffodil pots in the orchard's place
my woods have shrunk to a bay tree and
pheasants are finches.

I have grown to love my new kingdom
Weeds riots are easy to quash
storm attacks no longer scare me now
I control each inch of greenery.
Here I walk tall.

Sarah Williams (Tunbridge Wells)

You Can Do The Charleston At The Walpole Bay Hotel

Built in 1902 perched on the cliff tops of Cliftonville, Margate, Kent
There stands the seductress of this charm endowed hotel
With its wonderful bedecked veranda, antique olde world ballroom
Now owned by the visionary, gifted Bishop family
You may look out to sea and observe many a sail boat or freighter
On its way to London
The Walpole is loved by many, but probably not as much, as deeply,
as artist Tracey Emin who is doing what she can to assist
and raise funds for the veranda fund
Brian Eno and sculptor Anthony Gormley are frequent visitors too
Coming to this unique period citadel filled with furniture
and artefacts is it any wonder that this location is readily attractive
for photo shoots and well!
If you want your 15 minutes of fame you can be freely included
on the extras register
Why not venture into Thanet some day, come rain or shine
and visit the Walpole
Jolly good fun! Old chap!

Joy Sheridan (Westgate-on-Sea)

The World's Future in Our Hands

There'll be a time when the world comes crashing down,
The greediness of men is all it took; they just didn't play by the book.

Fuels and oils, power and gas,
all fought over by a crazy mass.

The world is desperate, the resources are out,
droughts are starting, famine is out.

The blame is always being passed,
from Amazon loggers to an Arabian oil mast.

But the true fact is we all share the blame,
and we all must act because,
the world will never be the same again.

George Horton (Sevenoaks)

Thailand

Land of a thousand smiles and as many smells.
Where the lotus blooms and mangrove mud bubbles
And pops in the midday heat.
Incense calms the mind and pungent drains assault one's nostrils.
Beauteous mountains dwarf the sweep of umbrella'd beaches -
Where white sand buries the condoms and bottles tops of last night.
Thirsty mynah birds grab a drink from chlorinated pools and
Hopeful tuk-tuks ply market streets for trade.
Bar-girls, pert and pretty, show slim legs in seedy dens
And painted 'he-girls' bewitch the curious.
Nothing here can be taken for granted!
Cross-legged lepers show sores and beg for bahts with empty mugs.
Turquoise seas stretch to the horizon and kindly breezes
Sway tall palms and stir the putrid rain.
Dogs curl up on pavements, unwashed, ungroomed,
Sporting great balls of fur and dangling dugs that trail the ground.
Nordic tourists tower over tiny Thais,
And Bin Laden grins from rows of T-shirts.
Motorbikes in endless processions, unhelmeted hordes
Of families travelling past;
And on sunbeds brown bodies soak-up the precious, lethal sun.
Thailand, pleased to see the strangers come,
Pleased to see them go
Back to their lands of sanitised living, pampered animals,
Endless rain and scowling faces.

Beneath the ocean many miles away, the land groans
And stretches, Tsunami is being born.

Yvonne Lane (Gillingham)

The Public Eye

I look around at the thriving streets,
In the centre of which my life revolves,
People swarming like ants,
To that which they desire.

They live their lives day by day
Conversing, working, shopping,
Bu unbeknownst to them they are watched,
Carefully, carefully, carefully.

Have you ever stopped and looked,
Above your life at the stars,
Winking slowly in a row,
Like millions of eyes.

Well I have looked at the stars,
I have also looked around from above,
To the point where all these eyes group,
To create the public eye.

We talk of dictators and evil people ruling the world,
We war against them through the years,
Hitler, Mussolini, Saddam Hussein,
But we always ignore the things around us.

I have seen the dictator,
Which rules our lives unseen,
I call it the Public Eye,
Because it sees all.

We say we are free,
Cleared of all restraints,
Yet we find ourselves changing,
To gain acceptance from the Public Eye.

You may not know it,
You may never know it,
But it is always there,
Watching, watching, watching.

I have seen how some suffer,
When they disobey,
Society turns on them and drives them to extremes,
And yet some do not change.

Maybe we are the wise ones,
Who show we're not afraid,
We do not cower under the Public Eye,
And its burning gaze.

I know it's a lot to grasp,
Like finding water you cannot hold,
Or discovering you were being followed,
On a long and lengthy road.

You must take heed of my warning,
Before you are consumed,
You don't have to obey the Public Eye,
Or change who you are to be accepted.

We are all meant to be different,
We are all meant to be unique,
The Public Eye loses power,
Whenever someone breaks free.

The chains it wields,
Are nothing more than paper,
Easily torn and shredded,
So break free.

Show you are not afraid,
Stand tall against the Public Eye,
Like we have to all dictators,
Drive it from hiding and from your lives.

Come and join the dissidents,
Push away its gaze,
You are stronger than you think,
And it is weaker than it knows.

I have said all that I wish to say,
The choice is now yours,
I cannot set you free,
I never could.

You must find who you are,
Before we are all the same,
Tear the chains and break the hold,
Before you ultimately pay.

Live your life the way you want and never obey the Public Eye . . .

Gareth Rayner (Maidstone)

Rievaul Abbey

Pigeon brothers,
perched high on ruined walls,
chant Matins through the winter silence;
clinking hammers add descant
and honking geese
a distant Angelus.

Discordant crows,
circling the dark wood,
caw in monotones,
momentarily breaking the pastoral peace
of a remote religious order,
preserved through lost centuries.

A black-robed nun
rakes up brown leaves
in sleeping garden of nearby cottage,
like an undertaker
caring for his dead,
giving service to the living.

Across the fields
two white goats,
mother and kid,
munching and milking,
mark out a smallholding
nestling in the land's immensity.

Men in denim overalls
work cheerfully;
ono with pipc and knitted cap
of monkshood blue -
more practical than
monkish hoods of old.

No tourists
but ourselves,
and only scaffolding to mar
an ancients abbey's beauty,
confirming man's essential art
in the eternal.

Mary Nugent (Whitstable)

Sonnet 1

I bent towards his lips; so soft and clean.
I looked into his eyes, so bright and wide.
Saw my reflection; deeper his soul seen,
His lips invite my kiss and stem the tide.
I bent towards his arms; my soul embrace -
His arms open wide - palms point to the sky.
No hint of silent shame, horror or debase.
Bend into his body - like new lovers fly.
Yet stop must I, before I too forget.
Not quench my thirst from overflowing springs.
Stop I must, before I start to regret.
See on my hand; two dulling golden rings.
No wrong have I done, nay my heart must save.
My husband only a year in his grave.

A M Williamson (Snodland)

Jesus Woz A Fascist

Jesus woz a fascist.
Muhammad was an alien.
Pretending they were born
From the Almighty's womb -
But that was their doom.

They preached the word of God
To everyone that could hear.
They were the chosen ones -
That was the priest's fear.

They journeyed across lands
To spread the Holy Word.
Many had turned a blind eye . . .
Shame they had to die.

When all was said and done
They returned to their Father.
Looking down at the gracious converted
Once again living their lives -
So they would go
Back to a heavenly paradise.

Jagdeesh Sokhal (Welling)

Polka Dot Days

Purple lupins, ten feet tall,
just a dream, just a wish,
beneath soft, pink apple blossom,
that floats like gossamer on the faintest breeze.
Happy days, happy times,
nurturing sweet peas to clamber across
grey, painted trellis, grey for effect,
worked well too.
So many sounds, touches,
emotions, today and always,
thinking of you, with your coal-black curls,
cat-green eyes and toffee apple smile.
Fun and laughter were your friends,
you taught them to be mine,
you showed me the beauty of the rose,
and what lies behind the thorns.
Each scarlet geranium takes me back
to the times when a little girl looked into
the rainwater tank, while you filled the can
that sometimes filled imaginary rivers.
You wore a polka dot dress, tightly grasped
by a broad, scarlet belt, you were my princess,
I wanted a dress like yours, to be so pretty,
just like you, my princess, my mum.
Even your shoes were scarlet leather,
cosseting dainty feet that loved to dance.
Laughter filled your life and mine,
and on the air the scent of Gingham perfume.
Gingham for week days, Tweed for Sundays,
a little bit here and a little bit there,
always my friend, always my mum,
this morning I thought I heard you calling.

Patsy Goodsir (Westerham)

Empire, Leicester Square

My house of dreams and fantasy, the Empire,
Leicester Square, facing a green garden,
Foliage and statues, home for pigeons.

Inside I sit in the dark absorbing
Pictures on the screen of goddesses and
Heroes, enacting our dreams of love and loss.

Exciting us with action, adventure,
Laughter and tears. Who has not sighed over
Casablanca, Gone With the Wind, Sleepless

In Seattle, danced with Fred and Ginger
In one's imagination or laughed at
Bob Hope and the Three Stooges, or sat in

Horror as the shark in Jaws moved in for
The kill? An organist opened the night's
Performance, followed by dancing girls! Yes,

We used to get value for our money'
Our dreams were stirred not shaken. Lost in
The dark and in the back row, we dreamed on.

Joyce Robson (London)

SELCHP

The name is where it all started - *SELCHP*
Let's think back to 1996
When I became mayor for a year:

I visited all Lewisham landmarks.
This is the place where the rubbish goes;
The three R's: reduce, reuse, recycle.

On the train to London, written on the wall,
The sign - South East London Combined Heat and Power;
SELCHP. It became our recycling plant.

Invented to help clean the environment;
All our litter collected and burnt.
I sit in the chair and pull the lever.

All rubbish is dumped in heaps;
Through the window I see trash swept in mounds,
Among the garbage a statue.

Too late to rescue, someone's treasure lost,
Burnt up in fire to convert it all
Into heat, power and light; that's magic.

Foqia Hayee (Bromley)

Stone Hovis

The name began the magic: Stonc Hovis.
Let's take a ball of wool and wind it back
Through labyrinths of years until I find

Myself, aged nine, passing again the house
Where like a crocheted cosy, soft grey stone
Has settled grimly on its fairy tales.

Above my head, engraved upon the wall
Stone Hovse, announced in antique lettering:
U read as V so Hovis it became.

It was a source of constant fear - and hope:
Surely one day a dragon or a troll,
Some giant with twenty eyes, three-headed snake,

A spider spitting fire, a shrieking witch,
Would howl and thunder through the blackened gate?
Or, maybe, if I pressed against the stone

A hidden door, a fairy door, might yield
To let me through to some magician's yard,
Where fairy flowers bloom on fairy trees?

The wool jerks tight, the years spring up to date.
I pass again the treasure chest of tales
And see, through adult eyes, a dull stone house.

Jill Tritton (London)

On Twickenham Bridge

Sitting in a traffic jam
I watched a feather fall.
I never saw the bird
flying over orange dawn.
Soft, feathery wing beats
releasing softer down.
He didn't see me;
earthbound, work bound, mind blank,
locked in glass and steel.
But he sent me
a soft, white message floating down
of freedom from my earthbound toil.

Charmian Goldwyn (London)

The Moment

Enjoy the moment when it's still on
For good memories I know, do endear the heart
And a time well spent never leaves the mind
Enjoy it to the fullest when it's still yours
'Cos in the twinkle of an eye it may be gone
And it's impossible to regain once a moment is lost
Oh yeah! I remember when you were born
I took on every moment to be your number one
'Cos every second with you was similar to none
Three point two seven pounds was what you weighed
You smiled as though you already knew I was there
Waiting patiently for you to come into the world.
Your mother was still hurting but she held you to her heart
Flashing back and trying hard to hold back the tears
No doubt it was that moment that captures it all
So cherish the moment when it's still on
Knowing that good memories do endear the heart
And a time well spent never leaves the mind.

Ademola Adio (London)

Golden Hill (Bristol)

Arriving at daybreak with ravenous diggers
They chewed up the black soil,
Spewed cement over the field,
Farted steel and concrete and plate glass;
Smothered the long, silver grasses;
Sealed off the stream,
Banished the myriad burrowing, scuttling,
leaping, squeaking, cowering -
Inhabitants of the hedgerow;
Divided the sky into neat squares.

Then came windows, ablaze with plastic,
The fumes, fast food,
The tyres, traffic jams,
Greed and grabbit,
Sharp heels stab-stabbing,
Hunger dozing in doorways,
Screeching, roaring, slamming, crashing,
Dashing, stunning, deafening -
Magnificat of moneychangers,
Technology triumphant.

But, listen carefully,
And you'll hear willowherb
Spearing between pavements,
Dandelions disporting in car parks,
Concrete crumbling,
Buddleias laughing on tower blocks,
Wild things waking, stirring, breeding, seeding, buzzing, humming -
And at night, down silent streets,
See a fox walk.

Jill Truman (London)

Four Am

The world is still
All that can be heard on the outside is silence
As the world sleeps
Not a passing car or bus
Disturbs the silence of the world

Suddenly the silence is pierced by a bird call
That resonates across
Who was the originator?
Nobody knows
Just a bird call in the distance
Presaging the waking of the birds
And the later dawn chorus of the world
But the silence
Into which the songbird speaks
Is warm and gentle
With the companionship of worlds
Waiting for life to begin

Of Earth again to burst
Into the life of the city
With the hustle and bustle
And the noise of the day's beginning
And the streets are deserted and empty
From the night before
But soon the city will wake again
And the morning rush will start
When noise will once again stalk the city.

Alasdair Sclater (London)

Errors Of Judgement

Or you could have done it differently, Mr Blair?
Instead of leaving us with all this pollution
You could have had a sensible, more effective green policy.
Arriving at 10 Downing Street, on the wrong foot,
Promising no corruption in your government,
You may as well have promised to move mountains.

What exactly are you doing about high teenage pregnancy?
Because whatever it is, it's not working!
Ever thought of educating them on the stresses of a newborn?
To stop them getting up night and day to a baby's yell.
Why must you inflame strike situations?
By saying 'We are not paying them any more money'
With that attitude, it's no wonder the country is in a state,
Just talk to them, listen and compromise.

Smoking has been killing millions for centuries,
Whether you are addicted to nicotine or not,
And it is only now you think of banning it in public places?
To say you were slow on the uptake, is an oversight too far.

How dim were you not to react to childhood obesity, earlier?
You know it is the parents and the NHS who pay,
Jamie Oliver showed you the right path to lay.
Yet, children still think of vegetables in a hostile way.

Why not drum into the young the value of education?
How it can give them a better start in life,
Opening up the window of opportunity,
And how it can solve practical problems.

Fifteen sailors captured by Iran, another blunder.
Did you learn nothing from Mr Blunket's escapades first time?
That you took him back into the Cabinet a second time,
Only to have him do more shady shenanigans!

Ali Sebastian (London)

The Tibetan Story

Somewhere far in Tibet
lived a woman.
She had no children, no close family.

She loved the place
where she was born.
Where her parents
met each other.

The people in the mountains
loved every day.
Her painting was
so interesting and personal.

She had no expensive clothes.
She made her own jewellery.
When she walked on the footpath
in her heart she carried happiness.

Martha Angelica (London)

Museum-Goer

She walks with good intention. Sky's a pale
lilac, ground hard. She's off the bus and down
to the warm drafts of the tube. The only
single men have their heads inches from the

football. She's in a part of London that
she doesn't know. The voices start - *where's your*
A-Z, this isn't safe, where's your friends?
Head up, she walks along a polluted

dual carriageway, nearly convinced it's
the right direction. It is. Inside, she's
glad of the people, the chatter of the
crowd. She smiles hopefully. Talks for longer

than others when buying her ticket. In
the ladies she studies the puckering
under her eyes. Ageing alone. Who could
she have asked to this new exhibition?

She looks at paintings and other people
for an hour or two. Stops watching herself.

Katrina Naomi (London)

The Mysterious Winds

One day I was taking a walk the wind it seemed to
Say, walk with me, for a mile, as I started thinking.

Is this good? As I came across this clearing, no more
Wind, I stand still, only seeing the great tree, the

Wood flowers perfume all around the woodland,
Birds sing their sweet song, I pity the rose that

Lost its colour, ever so light upon the woodland
Just above the rocky ground, the trees dancing

Gracefully on the wind, long for the river to flow
Endlessly toward the ocean, I waited for the same

Old faces, I waited for the wind to blow, but it didn't
Tell me which way to go, still my heart would sing,

The road I am on is no longer dark, I finally know
The way, I have to try to hide, I remember when this
World brought me down, You Lord Jesus put my
Feet back on the ground.

Imogene Lindo (London)

Trent Country Park

Named Trent, after Trento,
Estate of the wealthy,
Now part of a uni,
And golf club and sports fields,
Centre for animals.
Play area for children,
All that the citizens
Of Enfield could want.

There's Oak Wood and Church Wood,
Shaws Wood and Williams Wood,
Ride Wood and Moat Wood
With walks to enjoy.

There are thousands of oaks
Purposefully planted.
An avenue of limes
Along the straight drive.
Alders and sycamores,
Tough hornbeams and beeches,
And no end of others
Midst all the tall trees.

With squirrels abounding,
Woodpigeons and great tits,
And down in the gully
A fox passes by.
Just above the green grass,
Large dock leaves and flowers,
Skipper and moth flutter,
My presence them scares.

Through meadows and green fields
I wander at leisure,
'Neath sunshine and blue sky.
No cloud to be seen.
No sound of aeroplanes,
Or trains or road traffic,
But alone with my thoughts,
At peace with myself.

David Oliver (London)

The Bathroom

The bathroom, a place of peace and solace
a place where one can
retire after a hard day at work to sit in
peace and quiet and reflect
on the activities of the day

A place where one can soak in the bathtub
with a glass of red wine with
lighted candles on each corner of the bath
while soft music plays in the
background or where one can doze off without
a worry in the world

A place where one can give one's nipper
a bath with her screaming
with delight where one's nipper can
make bubbles in the bath with the
soapy water

A place where one can have a quiet
moment with one's nipper
tickle her, talk to her and
sing soft music
to her
and in a place so small
and beautiful
made of marble and tiled walls
and floors!

Joana Efua Sam-Avor (London)

September Serenade

Panic, why not panic?
Blue suit crumpled in a chair
lined by scattered magazines
of debs and society junkies

He gathered up the day
and went towards the door.
Remember turn the gas off,
mustn't kill the budgie.

Lines of people in the street
lined and scarred with waiting.
Ticket jammed, driver's wrath
passengers asleep.

Revolving door, a smiling face
gone at once and not remembered.
Desk at angles to the light,
coffee waiting, cold by now.

Talking, always talking,
faceless men shuffling papers
leering at the new PA,
fidgeting for lunch.

Flip board, even more statistics,
sales are down,
down, down,
down we go.

Ho, ho, ho
and here we are;
the basement mortals
spewing mud.

Mop the floor
your tears are there.
You know
there's biscuits upstairs.

John Francis (London)

After Mercer

Like Guy the gorilla from London zoo
You raged on the Berlin Wall
A dentist without moral obligation

Fills the gap of a nation longing for
Solitude, like a sort of wife
Outdoor ablutions of a closed down life

Bravely plodding on they sang and blindly
Murdered dead composers
With fiddle and sickle and one last drink

A nation gets the government they think
Will rise like opera
With a love-stained knife

A private man - a blood-red life.

Michael Wagg (London)

Don't Cry Jelena

(To my daughter Jelena)

The night of distanced world is slowly coming down
Moon shines, wakes in darkness
I can see an angel that lands
On the child's eyes, blue cornflower

In distance it echoes and silently rings
The fluttering angel's wing
Someone's eyes are crying.
White lily of the valley in tears
Don't cry Jelena,
Your childish face is sad

Life is all about hope and your dreams . . .
Like snowflakes white and soft
Spread your arms so they fall in your hands
All the stars of the far away world

Step bravely in this darkness, without fear
When underneath the night sky
Covers pollen of stars
Your tearstained, childish eyes

And dream. Dream how with your hair
You entangle shining violets
Moon's silk how it shines
On decorated aureoles of Heaven
Like your soul, childish, innocent and pure

And then . . . sing a song
To the turtledove's tune
It takes so little to achieve happiness
So spread your arms
Dance on your piece of sky

And the clouds above this world
Will be your soft pillow
Peaceful like the child's eye
When you soar far, far away . . .

Don't cry, Jelena!

Maria Deyana (London)

Hello Missing Person

You read about them going away
To some far off place. That child
You reared as a toddler. Her first
Steps, clutching your hand
With sticky fingers, are now
Taking her across the world
Without your support. A girl
Flirts in a Tokyo night club;
That photo of her, all blonde
And carefree. Look, I have
Discovered life, it says.
You're all asleep! Here's where
It's at. Behind the sanguine
Glimmer of her eye is the
Snap-shut wallet, mind and heart
Of some cool oppressor. But she
Smiles on unknowing, and you
Cling to this memory, as once
You clung to that tiny hand,
Hearing forever in your head
The old sound of baby laughter
As you vainly trace her last steps,
Last sightings, last suppers, unable
To believe someone has stolen her.
And she grows old in her own absence.
Gone, drowned, like Ophelia, drowned
In the smile that launched a thousand sorrows
Or the siren sounds from her tumbling hair.

Gloria Tessler (London)

Starfish

Green, orange, pink and blue starfishes washed upon the shore.
Close by are two-headed fishes - what growths for sciences!
The nuclear waves probably did it to them.
Perhaps it was so that we wouldn't have to paint or spray them -
Before hanging them up like stars.
Not the way for Mother Nature to plan it!
So who was off their planet;
Before, they too decided to go and fish,
In a hell of a big sea?

Colette Breeze (London)

Seven Years On

Seven years on,
From the millennium year,
In a bird's eye view;
Nine-eleven, three-eleven, seven-seven!
A world war against terrorism is on,
Amidst fear of pandemic from bird flu.
The United States of Europe is emerging,
But are we living in a big brother state?
So much surveillance and monitoring!
The spider's web is spun faster and broader,
With a pin-hole in the centre.
The snail mail is slowly dying,
Mobile phones and digital services boom.
Shopping is by chip'n'pin or online,
Yet so much acquired debt!
Are we becoming a nanny state?
Five portions of fruit and veg a day,
If only there was a butterfly effect!
There would be no nip'n'tuck or botox.
Four by four craze, despite congestion charge,
If only public transport were our oyster!
Smoking ban and ASBO's for yob culture,
Yet students have been struck with top-up fees!
Earthquakes unlike lightning do strike twice,
Boxing Day tsunami, hurricane Katrina,
Massive floods are becoming a trend!
In our state two tornadoes have touched down.
In a worm's eye view;
What would things be like,
Seven years from now?

Eunice Ogunkoya (London)

Even With My Imperfections

Take each tear that falls from my eye,
and hold it tight in your hand.

Take the very pain from my heart,
and hold it with tender care.

Take each tremble of my voice,
and capture the sound in your ear.

I am but human, even with my faults, will you love me still?

Take each thunder in my step,
and give me wings so I can fly.

Take each doubt of my mind,
and embed thoughts that are kind.

I am but human, even with my imperfections, will you love me still?

Take each wear of my bones,
and build a tower of strength.

Take each grey that will grow through my hair,
And draw a silver line.

Take the very scars of my soul,
and build a beautiful temple in which my spirit shall dwell.

Take the very imperfections,
and find the perfections I have too.

Some say love is blind, but true love can see straight through the
perfections and love the imperfections just as well.

Kimberley Donaldson (London)

Exquisite Sorrow

Seek to proclaim true nature
through beauty's sexual nurture,
unrequited paradox,
persistently underplayed stumbling blocks,
waiting for that spiritual fidelity,
need to grab that heart to borrow.

Six foot tall, wit and wisdom,
sensual arrival of intelligence,
destructive morals of extravagance,
seduced dreadfully by strange pleasure,
as a rule of charming leisure,
boyhood lies cannot exist,
when diving into honey abyss,
wild and adolescent enthusiasm.

Divided lives replace generosity,
blackmailed unexpectedly by childlike tragedy,
green had fallen from your outlawed clutches,
seek and you will find scattered matches,
from the pockets of the pretenders,
hope never surrenders.

Reason's demonstrated by grey,
true lust pours out of fear,
through open windows of golden day,
people stop, point and leer,
strange insight corresponds repented lies,
sorry always follows forgotten goodbyes.
In darkness you lost true hope,
even though he seemed to forget,
both believed in forever shame,
in the end he did not see his debt,
forgetting his own tragic blame,
years followed his hated breath,
for he had nothing but fear left,
together your souls elope.

Donna Moulding (Littlehampton)

The Secret Kiss

As the darkness slowly surrounded the day
We gossiped and enjoyed the time
But I never thought things would end up that way
Where I had the heart to say you were mine

I didn't want you to be anything else but a friend
You were not allowed to know what I really did feel
I didn't want our friendship to come to an end
Until that day when everything seemed so real

Suddenly, silence surrounded the dark
What you were thinking about I did ask
As I looked into your eyes I saw a deceiving spark,
'I want to kiss you,' you replied at last

I pretended what you said I did not hear
But just then my heart must have missed a beat
To say something back I did not dare
I tried to pretend it was all a joke even though I found it sweet

Not soon after your imagination became so true
A word to nobody I shall say about this
The truth shall always remain between me and you
Now hush . . . I shall write no more about the secret kiss

Sonila Reka (London)

Rogues

Sly, genial rogues on the prowl in a country restaurant,
no passable woman past her prime is safe from them.
Grey, windblown, spicy seawolves anchored to swaying bar stools,
their rough, bohemian beards conceal their double chins,
their cardigans display their muscular arms and chests
discreetly folding over their stubborn expanding waistlines.
Lone, cunning rogues, they fly an innocent public smile,
inviting a conversation or just a vague approval
of themselves and their companions, the odd adoring daughter
already past the age of girls they secretly fancy.

Just look at the subtle rogues as they deftly chat up the wives
and make the charmless husbands wince in embarrassed rage.
Sophisticated rogues, pretending to have no thought
beyond the amusing story at hand while offering a drink
of tenderness, of friendship and even a sense of importance
to lost and parched and wretched wanderers seeking a soulmate.
Poor rogues, squeezed by taboos attained in their former lives
allowing them to compete for fewer and fewer women:
the ones still older than their daughters, yet younger than
their wives who've grown beyond their reach and comprehension.

I watch you, rogues, as I take my table with my doting
young lady daughters in this family restaurant
and sadly contemplate the absence of my wives.
I am a good learner and no less a rogue and no more likely
to give up my animal grip on life than any of you.
I thus survey these shrinking hunting grounds and draw
engaging, furtive greetings from wives at distant tables.
A drink to you, my unwelcome brothers, a drink to life
and to simple truth admitted in crisp and relentless focus.
We are the final hope of graceful, middle-aged women.

Thomas Land (London)

Angels Can Fly

We are not of the flesh
But of another kind
To let our minds meander
And sometimes to entwine.

We are not of the mundane
Ground down by the daily grind
But souls soaring freely
This is where we combine.

We may never meet earthly
But this is far from fallen grace
I feel your heart touching me
And we'll meet in Paradise.

Susan Vango (Isleworth)

Musing About A Muse

I really could use a beautiful muse
to banish the blues, you just can't lose.
This is serious; it's no caper
I'll put an ad in the local paper:

WANTED: 18 year - 16 year old - ingénue,
svelte and French and of good virtue.
Sought by overweight man, 62,
linen clothes and ponytail hairdo.

Her name: Michelle and we'll live in sin.
Better still, she'll bring Simone, her identical twin.
We'll move to a chateau on the Cote D'Azur,
Renoirs on walls, feet slapping on floors
(You never wear shoes if you've taken a muse).
Bohemia, we'll choose, drinking loads of booze.
I'll read Sartre and J'Accuse, no curfews, no taboos.

Ah! But Michelle and Simone, I shall bemoan.
Our relationship will be blighted.
As you giggle and flirt in Laura Ashley skirt,
my love for you will be unrequieted.
Sunlit smiles as you snooze will inspire writing of gnus,
igloos . . . zoos . . . canoes . . . and tattoos.
The reviews! I'll be praised and berated,
irrelevant when you're sexually frustrated.

Unfulfilled, I shall die; mon cherie will be bereft.
I'll just check with Mr Perkins if I've any holiday left.

Richard Mathews (Oxford)

The Ridgeway

There is a favourite place where I escape sometimes.
This ancient, green road runs towards the west
from Chilterns to Berkshire downs to Wiltshire green
(but never in the other direction!)
Here I can find peace and joy and beauty
in solitude and quiet, never loneliness,
and lift my spirit up to higher spheres.
All I can hear are breezes through the trees,
great clumps of beech that stand aloof and dark.
A skylark rises over cornfields, song aloft,
hovering above a nest so well concealed,
that I must tread more carefully than usual.
Here and there a glimpse of deer or hare
show perfect harmony of form and colour.
Only a distant fleeting train that snakes
through chequered fields below, returns one's mind
to reality of ongoing living and the daily grind.
To the far west, the glorious comforting Cotswolds;
to north, blue misty views over Oxford's Shotover.
Sometimes I meet an earnest, back-packed man
with muddy, well-worn boots and sturdy stick.
Exchange of nods and cheery morning smiles
sufficient - humans are irrelevant up here!
The early drovers with their woolly flocks
were first to use this ancient English road,
now rutted, full of rain in winter, mud in spring,
and fringed with narrow strips of splashed, worn grass,
while further back, long copses where the pheasants hide,
and wild things undisturbed, get on with life.

Joan Carter (Abingdon)

Flowers In The Rain

Love shines
with an unseen radiance,
seemingly destined
to last for eternity.

Fathomless hearts
now filled to overflow,
warmth and softness,
minds and souls dance on air.

How long
will love's sweet flower
blossom and retain
its beauty and sweetness?

As sure
as day turns into night,
yet unforeseen
bitterness will follow close behind.

Anguish is
creeping ever closer,
that delicate flower
will be crushed underfoot.

Warm tears
will soon be falling
from beautiful eyes,
like flowers in the rain.

Marisa Greenaway (Abingdon)

Coventry Cathedral

Love
And stillness
In my heart,
The atmosphere
Of the cathedral
Set me apart,
Yet I belonged.
Spiritual peace
And tranquillity
Beyond comprehending
Invaded, pervaded
My soul,
My heart
They
Became
Lighter, happier.
The bonding,
The union
Of the burnt
Skeleton
Of St Michael's,
With the new
Was overwhelming.
A powerful sense
Of the nearness
Of our Creator
Lay
In these buildings.
As well
As awe,
The strength
Of belief
In the omnipotent one.

The images of Jesus
And of God
Expressed in so many different ways,
Forms,
Brick, stone,
Wood, silver,
Gold, glass
And marble.
A boulder
From Bethlehem.
All blending
In perfect
Harmony
Into the form,
The substance
Of the cathedral.
Its architectural
Splendour
And symmetry
Mingled with
Simplicity.
Passion, love
And thoughtfulness
Reigned
In this beautiful creation
I had come to see.
This, I believe
Was my reward.
Reconciliation
The theme
And peace
On Earth
For evermore.
Would it were so
Today.

Patricia L Laing (Taunton)

Into The Darkness

Tears run, tasting of salt
can only a memory sustain
sighed anguish of remorse
the light dims on the chastened soul.
Days of rain barred an exit
pressed into servitude the will gave way
understanding was called for
but could not be found
the essence of the words remained lost.
Dress warmly in the emotions
that linger in your mind.

Katrina Warren (Oxford)

The Beach

Cold,
Wet,
Not alive,
Asleep,
And the
Horizon
In the
Distance.

No
Sun,
Not much fun,
Unlike the road journey,
Supernaturally cold,
Off-season.

Nicola Barnes (Taunton)

Liffey

As a mere boy in nineteen fifty-nine
Twelve, going on thirteen years old,
Sunday walks along the Liffey bank
I watch the vein of my Dublin flow.
She was the Amazon of my youth
The longest river I'd seen or known,
Her pungent smell was sweet to me
It was the smell of my own Dublin.

She was the shire horse of my youth
The lungs that made Dublin breathe,
The smell of seaweed and salted iodine
Hid the swallowing smell the city leaves.
Often I watched her breast rise and swell,
Lapped at the stone boundary of the quays,
Die back at the evening tide and in her
Shimmering lit dress she was a queen.

She was a biddy like any other Dublin biddy,
Whose moods and changes were many.
Splash and spray at the passer-by,
Especially on a beautiful windy day.
She was the heart that drove the city,
The secret that makes the Guinness taste.
Matchmaker that never spoke a single word
But sealed the future happiness of many.

As wide as O'Connell Street, without
Monument on her watery thoroughfare,
Life in its cosmopolitan fashion passes
Over her legs as if her city is a giant fair.
Dublin lives as if there is no tomorrow,
Her weather beaten face always happy,
Whatever her magic it must be the sweet Liffey
That makes her the colleen most snappy.

You heard of the hawker sweet Molly Malone
Selling her fruit from a cart in the road,
Moore Street, infamous as the River Liffey
Where the craic was the banter, with the sellers,
The newsboys shout till their voices croaked
Each trying to out-scream each other.
But for all that magic that is the theatre of street,
None compare with my ageless, sweet Liffey.

Philip A McDonnell (Camberley)

Home Again

Isn't it good to go home again,
To your friendly, nervous greeting,
I'm nervous too,
Not having seen you in ages.
Chatter and into the brightly lit kitchen
Where once I used to sit.
Nothing seems to have changed,
Apart from the new microwave.
Now into the front room,
With the warm fire burning,
Cat curled up on the sofa,
You look pleased to see me.
The power within is amazing,
So frail, you manage the house well.
A cup of tea and biscuits
And the latest gossip - non-stop chatter,
As gradually my soul comes together.
I almost forget . . . here's some chocolates.
Talk about Dad - she's lonely for him,
I miss him too.
As the tears and the years roll away,
We are at peace with each other.
Our anguished hearts mended.
I like being here,
You're my mother;
Isn't it good to come home again?

Derek Harris (Weston-Super-Mare)

The Surrey Hills

I walked along a hill top path
With my old dog Jake
Beneath a cloudless sky of azure blue
The path led me into a sparsely wooded copse
Its leafy canopy defused the strong sun
And provided welcome shade
I decided to rest a while in the cool shadows
I slipped off my back pack
And sat against a tree's trunk
I wiped the sweat from my brow
Before taking my bottle from my pack
I poured water into a bowl for Jake
And took a generous swallow for myself
Then I lit my pipe and relaxed
In an aromatic cloud and enjoyed the scene
Specks of sunlight dappled the ground
And midges danced around the sunbeams
As Jake chased the shadows
The time came to move along
And we followed the path back into the sun
And onward along the ridge
After a long, slow crawl up the ever steepening path
We reached the summit and were duly rewarded
To see the countryside stretching far to the south
Spread like a great patchwork quilt
This perfect view from the Surrey Hills.

Paul Curtis (Woking)

My Lover

Your eyes sparkle, when you look into my eyes
Your smile lights up my life.
Time stands still when you look into my eyes
Your kiss sets me on fire, you touch my body I'm aflame
You were there all the time
And I didn't see, you care for me
You are life as I am a free spirit
Our love is magic, I want to be with you in every romantic place
Sunsets, waterfalls, pools of light
I think of you by day and night
We have such fun in wind and sun
I hope we will always be this way
Please say you'll stay.

Valerie Harris (Cheam)

No Puede Lire

'I can't see to thread a needle'
and
'I can't read' -
A phrase from 75% of patients!

Reading glasses are
Such a simple thing!
But our work seems
To be a drop in the ocean

In a country where,
Despite reclassification as
A middle income country,
The gap between the rich and the poor
Expands

And I doubt the statistics
As I see little change
In rural quality of life

Lack of vision
Seems to be something
Not just experienced
By the elderly poor!

Natalie Jagger (Godalming)

The High Street

Cold cobbles line the passageways;
Monuments of centuries past,
when horseback rode, instead of hustling hordes.

Tradesmen sell their wares;
Silver lockets, famous faces,
stamped on plastic mats,
and stoned musicians striving for success.

Decadence abounds;
fashion chains fighting for fortune,
epitomising avarice, achieving their aim,
whilst beggars sit, unnoticed,
amidst the throng of indifference.

Busy, bustling, absorbed,
the crowd progresses;
each member oblivious to the rest,
locked in a microscopic world.

Teenagers swagger in sets,
defiant, aggressive,
angst on the faces of myriad mothers.

Lovers stroll, assured and boasting,
dressed in jeans and jackets.

Rails of clothes stores
hang in colourful disarray.
Shelves of bookstores carelessly rearranged.
Cafés welcome weary wanderers
with tempting treats; shoppers' respite.

The town hall clock strikes six
and the multitude disperses.

The High Street stands shell-shocked,
from invasion by the masses.

Caroline Baker (Guildford)

Broken Soul

A young woman looks out to sea
The waves crashing against the pier
And a wild wind
She hides a secret within
Tormented by her childhood
She is a broken soul
Looking to be reborn
And learn to live again
The violence of the sea gives her strength
And hope in her lonely heart
And she now knows she can make it through
And no longer be afraid.

Jenna Fry (Farnham)

Fantasies Of A Child

When I was just a little girl
Which now seems so long ago
I'd dream of making footprints
In the pure, fresh fallen snow
And I'd often dream of angels
Pretending I was one
Giving out love so serene
To each and everyone
But, alas, my childhood dreams
Were just silly fantasies
A child with hopes and dreams
Trying just to please
And I really tried so desperately
To be a good little girl
But late at night I sobbed in bed
My fantasies turned to hell
And in the light of my cold, dark days
Angels were not true
They didn't come to rescue me
When I was beaten black and blue
Nor could I walk through pure snow
Because I was so bad
Naughty girls didn't do nice things
They just made daddies mad
But now I'm much older
And dying in my warm bed
And there right beside me
Is an angel at my head
And in her eyes there's sorrow
For what she cannot change
Can't give me a tomorrow
And for the past there's no exchange
But when I get to Heaven
I promise I'll try to be
The nicest little girl ever
Just to please my mad daddy.

T Simpson (Carshalton)

Paper Smile

Turn around, move back to your sound
dust yourself apart
Reflected sunlight making shapes on the wall
I think that's all you are to me
Use your see-through eyes to get your own way
asking where are you now
suggested love meaning pieces for all
retro wonder on the outside

fenced out nightmare knocking on the door
falling on your life
is there anyway you could get here to me
it's not the same without you
I can't hear you when you're shouting so loud
it's just ouija talk to me
paper smile meaning nothing to you
follow the old roads home.

Daniel T Morgan (Sutton)

Marine Park Gardens, Aldwick

The gardens are a-dance
With newly planted flowers.
The putting green awaits,
New mown and freshly rolled.
These gardens are my solace
And my joy in times of leisure.
I walk here everyday and bless
The gardeners who strive
To give the public pleasure.

Christina Stowell (Bognor Regis)

Newtimber Hill

The Weald was choked in clinging murk,
The Downs stretched up the chalky steep
Submerged in swathes of miry clay;
The trees like ghosts about my path
Let fall their droplets in my hair.
The muggy air was breathless, still,
As I climbed upward swathed in gloom;
The deadened silence wrapped me round,
No sound from birds too glum to sing.

I slithered on the slippery slope,
Then climbed the stile and left the wood
To feel my mood to lighten some.
The mist still clung to sodden grass
As I resumed my weary climb.
But suddenly the gloom was gone
And sunshine bathed the landscape, while
The golden gorse was scattered wide
And spiders strung their diamonds there.

The sky stretched round in deepest blue
With larks ecstatic, hovering there -
I revelled in this fairyland.
Below, the tower of Poynings church
Just pierced the clouds that hid the nave,
Reminder of the certain hope
That lifts the soul beyond the tomb
And out into the sunlight, where
The fresher air excites the breath.

Winter and Spring have hastened by
And Summer still extends its reign
As I climb nimbly through the shade.
The Weald below is bright and clear
And Wolstanbury bathes in light
As does the hill to westward, which
Is cleft in two by Devil's Dyke.
Silence, peace, relaxing space -
My favourite place, Newtimber Hill.

Vaughan Stone (Burgess Hill)

Binsted Wood

Down Tortington Lane three heads graze,
Muzzles soft upon the stubble.
The slightest sound and antlers lift,
Alert to the sense of trouble.

Beyond the spray of blackberry,
Its lobes of dark, alluring fruit,
Lies the gloom of Binsted Wood
Where deer roam and owls hoot.

A secret vista, a sudden surprise
Beyond the hips and hazelnuts,
The deer take flight and plunge where
Pigeons flap and pheasants strut.

The young of spring all a-twitter,
The heat of summer in its fury,
Give way at last to autumn calm
And Binsted Wood reveals its story.

Deep in this fecund, fertile world
Many followed the lover's call;
Tender memories comforting
When age's cloak does fall.

Beneath the blood-red necklace
Of deadly nightshade festooning,
Molten streams run white-hot but once
Till lava black begins its silting.

Scabs cover, but the heat of pain
Flows under fern fronds that unfurl
Erect to another verdant spring,
But our love doth winterwards swirl.

So? Are there ghosts in Binsted Wood?
Yes. Ghosts of love that could not stay.
The discreet earth will never say,
Only the trees know we passed this way.

Joan Woolley (Arundel)

What Is Death?

Death is nothing at all I have only slipped next door
I and you are whatever we were to each other, that we still are
Call me by my old familiar name,
Speak to me in the easy way you always use too,
Put no differences into your tone,
Wear no frown of solemnity or sorrow,
Laugh as we always laughed at the jokes we enjoyed together
Play, smile think of me,
Let my name be the household name it always was,
Let it be spoken without effort, without the ghost of a shadow on it
Life means all it is ever meant, it is the same as it always was,
There is absolutely unbroken continuity,
What is death but a negligible accident
Why should I be out of mind or sight,
Until we meet again may God hold you in the hollow of His hand
Until we meet again on that bright, golden shore
In a land where we shall never part
O Father of eternal life and all created glories under Thee,
Resume this spirit from this world of pain and death
Into Your mansion of peace and true liberty.

John Mason (Trowbridge)

So Near And Yet So Far

A voice called out, I looked around
who was that I asked, my friends about me said
it wasn't us, it must be in your head
but the voice kept on, it troubled me
I could not place it - yet - I knew its
sound. As days went by I heard it often
when I was quiet and still, I asked around
if anyone knew of someone gravely ill
but no one knew, yet I could not set my mind at rest.

The weeks went by, the voice began to fade,
still there but I pushed it into the recess
of my brain, but then I received a letter,
my first love, she was very ill, she I had
also loved so many years before
I had to go and find her, before it was too late,
and I was halfway around the world and she
in Devon, England, even now it was too late.

A full month it took me to reach old
England's shore, and race by horse and carriage
across unfriendly moors.
When I arrived, straight to her bed I strode,
She opened her eyes and whispered,
'I can go now, for I have called for you for so long.'
She squeezed my hand and then was gone.

Howard Gibbs (Marlborough)

Life On A Housing Estate

I have a dream that I'll move to the country,
Swapping minimalistic for gingham and lace,
Collecting firewood and perhaps making chutneys
And enjoying life at a steadier pace.

But the reality is I live on a housing estate,
Where the houses are built back to back,
When I relax in the garden it's in full view of the block,
Yes its' privacy that I lack.

Then there's the unrestrained shouting
Coming out of the houses reflecting the turmoil within,
They will argue in the street if they feel so inclined,
It doesn't matter to them if they're seen.

I hear screaming and swearing in the 'wee' early hours
and if sometimes I dare to peep out,
I will see staggering figures making their way back to their homes
After another late night drinking bout.

So I shut them all out when I close my fron t door,
I can pretend that they're not really there,
Perhaps one day I'll move to the country
And turn my back on all this and not care.

Eileen Wilby (Chatham)

Smarden Charter Hall

(New Hall built and opened January 2007)

Past, present and future
beautifully woven
in the very fabric and building
speak warmly already
as we enter the 'hop pocket' area -
welcoming, light and spacious,
with a mini 'gallery' of interest on its walls,
not to be missed.

The oak floor alone
embraces past, present and future
magnificently.
Raise your eyes
and the acoustic tiled roof
certainly is uplifting -
every time you walk into the main hall.
Quality, simplicity and style blend softly.
Meticulous thought to detail everywhere,
bringing a sense of real pleasure.

Another rare treat is the 'gift' dream kitchen!
'Dadson' and 'Turner' rooms,
provide dual purposes
efficiently.
Quite exceptional stage and lighting facilities
are breathtaking.
Charter Hall nestles in the corner neatly
with a real flavour of Kent and the Weald about it,
expressing all that is unique
about village life, and spirits soar here.
Generosity, teamwork,
first-class professional dedication
at all times -
a community achievement
without parallel anywhere.

Margaret Ann Wheatley (Ashford)

Untitled

The streets to me are a cage. Oppressive.
Tendrils veer off in all directions, winding and connecting,
urging hesitant steps along.

I walk along most days and find it hard
to recollect anything at all;
familiar faces, places, words and ideas could pass me by,
and I'd never know. No,
I go round this particular city numb and inarticulate.

I find that faces terrify me,
my own face terrifies me. All pockmarked with bloodshot eyes,
the thought of people looking at my face terrifies me.

People' talking scares me too. Sometimes, most times,
I don't want to talk. Let me communicate
by passing notes around,
maybe then my handwriting will improve.

The pleasures of the imagination don't occur as I walk,
no, they wait and bombard me at home, they can be quite cruel,
and the stillness, the silence of the mind is not always welcome.

But each day I try, and each day I fail
in writing something I consider good,
as I sit in my new backdrops, among new people,
I feel compelled to write of reasons why I detest these places,
this clutter of souls.

Not always. Sometimes I hope someone will stop and talk.
In public places I can feel so lonely, so bereft it's painful.
But please don't let me whine, don't let me beg.

I don't have time for this, I just don't have the time.
The minutes of my life ebb away so quickly and I worry.
I do not want to lose all hope.
I always wanted a full life.

J Russell (Whitstable)

Poetry Now Information

We hope you have enjoyed reading this book - and that you will continue to enjoy it in the coming years.

If you like reading and writing poetry drop us a line, or give us a call, and we'll send you a free information pack.

Alternatively if you would like to order further copies of this book or any of our other titles, then please give us a call or log onto our website at www.forwardpress.co.uk

Poetry Now Information
Remus House
Coltsfoot Drive
Peterborough
PE2 9JX

(01733) 898101